WARRIOR SCIENCE

GLADIATOR
Science

Armor, Weapons, and Arena Combat

by Allison Lassieur

Consultant:
Josh Davis
Historian and Craftsman
Davis Reproductions
St. Paul, MN

CAPSTONE PRESS
a capstone imprint

Edge Books are published by Capstone Press,
1710 Roe Crest Drive, North Mankato, Minnesota 56003
www.mycapstone.com

Library of Congress Cataloging-in-Publication Data
Names: Lassieur, Allison, author.
Title: Gladiator science : armor, weapons, and arena combat / by Allison Lassieur.
Description: North Mankato, Minnesota : Capstone Press, [2017] | Series: Warrior science |
    Includes bibliographical references and index. | Audience: 8–12. | Audience: 4 to 6.
Identifiers: LCCN 2015049407 (print) | LCCN 2016004051 (ebook) | ISBN
    9781491481295 (library binding) | ISBN 9781491481455 (eBook PDF)
Subjects: LCSH: Gladiators—Juvenile literature.
Classification: LCC GV35 .L37 2017 (print) | LCC GV35 (ebook) | DDC 796.8—dc23
LC record available at http://lccn.loc.gov/2015049407

Summary: Describes the science behind the armor, weapons, training, and tactics
used by gladiators in combat.

Editorial Credits
Aaron Sautter, editor; Steve Mead, designer; Pam Mitsakos, media researcher;
Steve Walker, production specialist

Photo Credits
Alamy: INTERFOTO, 19, Jochen Tack, 21; Bridgeman Images: Bianchetti/Leemage, 26, De
Agostini Picture Library/G. Dagli Orti, 24–25, Look and Learn, 13; Dreamstime: Microstock77,
cover background, 22–23 bottom background; Getty Images: Ann Ronan Pictures/Print Collector,
29, Doug Pearson, 10, Nicolas Moulin Photography, 9, Prisma/UIG, 5; iStockphoto: oscar_killo, 28,
Sylphe_7, 17 top right; Newscom: akg-images/Peter Connolly, 16 bottom middle, Photo by Guy
Bell/REX Shutterstock (4931217ba), 8; Shutterstock: 3drenderings, 17 left, bkp, right cover,
Dmytro Zinkevych, left cover, 11, Eky Studio, cover background, design element throughout book,
Fotokvadrat, 23 top, Luis Louro, 6–7, back cover, Nebojsa Kontic, cover bottom left, 22, Nejron
Photo, 14–15, Paul B. Moore, cover bottom middle, Prapann, 16 middle right, Santi0103, cover
bottom right; Thinkstock: Klemen Misic, cover top middle

Printed and bound in China
PO007733LEOF16

TABLE OF CONTENTS

SCIENCE: TO THE DEATH!

The two gladiators stood face to face. Their bodies dripped with sweat and blood. The men circled each other, careful to avoid the slick, dark blood from earlier battles. Each warrior sized up his opponent … when would he make his move? How hard would he hit? Which way would be best to dodge when he attacks?

Suddenly one man lunged forward to attack. But he leaned in too far and lost his balance. Unfortunately, his opponent saw the mistake. He slashed the stumbling warrior with a lightning-fast sword strike. The unlucky gladiator went down in a pool of blood. The Emperor smiled as the victorious warrior waved to the crowd.

For Roman gladiators, success in combat depended on more than strong weapons. Science was just as important as a sharp sword. For the winning warrior above, speed was a deciding factor. Being faster than his opponent helped him achieve victory. Ancient Roman gladiators relied a lot on science during their battles. Using the science behind their weapons and combat skills often meant the difference between life and death.

To survive and succeed in the arena, Roman gladiators relied on the science behind their armor, weapons, and combat training.

CHAPTER ONE

PROTECTED BY SCIENCE

Gladiators knew every day could be their last. Two things stood between them and death: their armor and science. Gladiators may not have realized it, but they relied a lot on the **physics** of their armor in battle.

Staying Alive with Physics

A gladiator's armor was his first line of defense. Metal armor didn't just keep a warrior from getting cut with a sword. When a weapon hit a gladiator's armor, the blow released a lot of energy. The armor worked to **disperse** that energy across its surface so the warrior's body didn't absorb it. Most armor was also made with smooth, rounded shapes that helped **deflect** weapons. This design made it difficult for enemies to connect with a solid blow.

physics—science that studies matter, energy, force, and motion

disperse—to spread out over a wide area

deflect—to cause something to go in a different direction

Gladiators also carried shields made of bronze or iron. Their shields were great at blocking and deflecting heavy blows from strong weapons. A skilled gladiator could even use his shield to knock an opponent off balance, which gave him a big advantage in a fight.

Heavy shields were also useful for absorbing and dispersing the energy from weapon blows.

Heavyweight Gladiators

Gladiators were divided into heavyweight and lightweight classes based on their size and strength. Heavyweight gladiators included *secutors* and *murmillos*. They wore metal armor and carried large shields. Their heavy armor provided good protection. But it slowed them down and exposed them to attacks from faster opponents.

SECUTOR

SECUTOR MEANS "CHASER." THIS HEAVY GLADIATOR'S JOB WAS TO CHASE DOWN AND DEFEAT HIS OPPONENTS BEFORE HE BECAME TOO TIRED.

HELMET
The secutor's helmet was smooth and round. It included a wide guard that protected the fighter's neck. But the helmet's small eyeholes made it difficult to find an opponent during combat.

MANICA
Manicas helped protect the warriors' sword arms.

OCREA
These leg guards covered a warrior's knees and shins.

MURMILLO

HELMET

The big fin-like crest helped deflect blows to the head. The full-face grill protected the fighter's face from the sharp prongs of an opponent's trident.

SCUTUM

This big, curved shield was made from three layers of wood glued together and covered with leather. It was strong enough to deflect powerful blows from almost any weapon. But its 22-pound (10-kilogram) weight slowed gladiators down.

MANICA

A manica could be made of leather, cloth, or metal. It was worn on the warrior's sword arm for protection.

OCREA

This metal leg guard covered the warrior's knee and shin. It protected the front of the gladiator's leg that wasn't covered by the scutum.

BALTEUS

This wide leather or metal belt was the only body protection these gladiators were allowed to wear. It protected a warrior's midsection from enemy weapons.

9

Lightweight gladiators included the *hoplomachus* and *retiarius*. These warriors carried few weapons and wore little armor. This exposed them more to attacks from heavily armored opponents. But their light gear allowed them to run fast and make nimble attacks.

RETIARIUS

RETIARIUS MEANS "NET-FIGHTER." THESE GLADIATORS GOT THEIR NAME FROM THE WEIGHTED NETS THEY USED DURING BATTLES.

BAREHEADED

This gladiator type was the only one to go bareheaded into battle. By not wearing a heavy helmet, these fighters had great vision and could quickly dodge attacks. However, a single well-aimed blow could kill them.

GALERUS

This shoulder guard protected a fighter's left shoulder and upper arm. The metal absorbed the energy of a blow, while the curved upper plate helped deflect attacks.

BALTEUS

This wide leather belt helped protect a fighter's midsection from stabbing and cutting attacks.

MANICA

Swords and other sharp weapons could easily cut through leather manicas. To solve this problem, some gladiators boiled the leather in water and wax to make it harder and stronger.

HOPLOMACHUS

HELMET

The hoplomachus' helmet had a rounded top and wide, low brim. Its design helped deflect an enemy's sword before it could cause damage.

BALTEUS

This wide leather belt protected a fighter's midsection during battle.

MANICA

Like other gladiators, the hoplomachus wore a manica to protect his sword arm.

PARMULA

Hoplomachus gladiators fought with these small, round shields attached to their left arms. They were small, but strong and useful for deflecting blows.

OCREA

Because of their small shields, these gladiators needed better leg protection. They often wore padded wraps under metal plate armor. The metal plates helped deflect sword strikes, while the padding helped absorb the energy of a blow.

CHAPTER TWO

DEATH BY SCIENCE

Gladiators were trained in various fighting styles and used specific weapons for those styles. Their weapons used science in different ways to be effective in battle.

Heavy vs. Light Weapons

Heavyweight gladiators used mostly heavier weapons like swords and spears. The fighters knew how to use these weapons to create maximum **momentum** in an attack. When they hit another object they created a heavy impact that could cause a lot of damage.

Lightweight gladiators relied on weapons that allowed for speed and **mobility**. Lightweight weapons like daggers could stab, thrust, and cut quickly and effectively. Using these weapons, a lightweight fighter could make fast, deadly attacks before his opponent could strike back.

momentum—the amount of force in a moving object determined by the object's mass and speed

mobility—the ability to move quickly and easily

FACT

Most gladiators carried more than one weapon. If a warrior lost his main weapon, a smaller one was used as a backup. Small weapons were good for close combat too.

As with armor, a gladiator's weapons were based on his weight class. Heavy weapons were strong and could do great damage. Light weapons were easy to handle and could be used to strike quickly.

THE *GLADIUS*

THE MOST FAMOUS WEAPON OF THE GLADIATOR WAS THE *GLADIUS*. THIS SHORT SWORD WAS USED MOSTLY BY HEAVYWEIGHT GLADIATORS. ITS KILLER REPUTATION CAME FROM THE SCIENCE OF ITS DESIGN. THE SWORD'S WIDE, THICK BLADE HELPED REDUCE THE AMOUNT OF **FORCE** NEEDED TO CUT THROUGH AN ENEMY. ITS SHORT LENGTH ALSO MADE IT EASY TO USE IN CLOSE COMBAT.

BLADE TIP

When stabbing with the gladius, the force of the blow was concentrated in the tip of the blade. This concentrated energy allowed the blade to pierce the enemy's armor and body.

BLADE WIDTH

The gladius' wide shape helped make it stronger and less likely to get bent in a fight.

BLADE LENGTH

The gladius' short length required a gladiator to add strength and speed to get a killing blow. Heavyweight fighters used their own strength, **mass**, and arm speed to give the sword the necessary momentum for the kill. But lightweight gladiators had to run at an opponent to get the greatest momentum possible.

The word "gladiator"
comes from the name
of the sword, gladius.

force—energy or strength

mass—the amount of material in an object

Weapon Science

Gladiators used many kinds of weapons for arena fighting. Some weapons relied on weight and momentum to strike a deadly blow. Others were dangerous because of their speed and ability to quickly deal damage.

BOW AND ARROW

Sagittarius gladiators often fought with bows and arrows. A bow is a simple machine called a "two arm spring." When a warrior pulled back on the bowstring, the force was stored as **potential energy**. When he let go of the string, the energy became **kinetic energy** to let the arrow fly to its target.

SICA

The *sica* was a short, curved sword. Its blade was about 16 to 18 inches (41 to 46 centimeters) long. It focused the force of a blow into a small area. The curved shape also provided a better angle of attack, allowing more of the blade to hit the target.

NET AND TRIDENT

These were the weapons of retiarius gladiators. Heavy lead weights were knotted into the ropes of the net. When the retiarius threw the net, the weights increased the net's momentum to help it fly faster and farther.

Spearlike tridents were used for piercing enemies' bodies or poking out eyes. One prong was longer than the other to focus the force of a thrusting strike. Tridents were about 6 feet (1.8 meters) long. Their length allowed retiarius warriors to slash and cut at enemies from a greater distance.

SPEARS

Spears worked best at high speed. Gladiators gave a spear speed in two ways. One was by running while holding it. The faster he ran, the more force he could use to thrust the spear into his enemy. Gladiators sometimes threw spears instead. A warrior used his strength to hurl it with as much force as possible. The harder he threw the spear, the faster and farther it traveled.

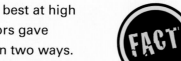

FACT

Sometimes a gladiator's sword was purposely blunted before a fight. It takes more force to cut with a dull blade. This made the fight longer and more interesting for the crowds.

potential energy—energy stored in an object, waiting to be released

kinetic energy—the energy of a moving object

CHAPTER THREE

TRAINING TO LIVE AND KILL

Weightlifting. Sprints. Running. Jumping rope. Modern athletes train with these exercises all the time. Gladiators did too. Gladiator training was all about physical fitness. They focused on improving their **agility**, strength, and speed. They had to be in peak physical condition. Anything less meant almost certain death in the arena.

Weight Class Training

Gladiator trainees were divided based on their size. Large men were chosen to be heavyweight gladiators. They increased their strength and built muscle by lifting and carrying heavy objects. Other exercises included picking up other gladiators and swinging them around.

Smaller men usually became lightweight gladiators. These fighters focused on increasing their speed and endurance. They ran sprints, shadowboxed, and hit bags filled with sand. They also practiced their accuracy by throwing and catching a small ball while running.

agility—the ability to move in a quick and easy way

Daily Training

Gladiators began their training by learning to wrestle each other. They learned grapples, holds, takedowns, and other moves. Later they learned weapon skills by practicing with wooden weapons. As their skills improved, they gradually moved up to training with real swords, spears, tridents, and other weapons.

Regardless of their class, all gladiators trained to be stronger. Trainers used the idea of progressive overload to increase the warriors' strength. This type of training is done by gradually lifting more weight a little at a time. Over time the gladiators' muscles grew in strength and **stamina**.

Gladiators also needed to be able to move in combat. Agility and flexibility could mean the difference between victory and defeat. Trainees practiced with a special machine that had high and low rotating poles. They had to jump and duck to avoid getting their heads or legs bashed by the poles. This training helped them to have faster reflexes during a fight.

FACT

Gladiators had their own energy drink. It was made from ashes and vinegar. This mix had a lot of calcium, which was believed to help remedy body pain.

stamina—the energy and strength to keep doing something for a long time

Putting Training to the Test

Gladiators needed good balance to be effective fighters. Every object has mass and a **center of gravity**. A human's center of gravity is usually slightly higher than the waist.

Nutrition was an important part of gladiator training. Gladiators ate mostly beans and grains. This protein-rich food helped them become strong and gave them the energy they needed for fighting.

SPEAR THROWING SCIENCE

Spears were useful weapons for gladiators. They allowed the warriors to attack opponents from a safe distance. Accurate spear throwing involved physics, as well as strength, agility, good balance, and good aim.

1. The gladiator first judged the distance needed to throw the spear. Then he ran a short distance before throwing it. This added speed to the spear as he threw it, allowing it to travel farther.

center of gravity—the point at which a person or object can balance

A heavyweight gladiator learned to keep his center of gravity low by crouching or bending his knees. From this position he could move and attack without losing his balance. But a lightweight gladiator had to be fast on his feet while keeping his balance. Agility training helped him to control his center of gravity and maintain his balance during a fight.

2 A gladiator had to throw a spear with the correct angle of attack to hit the target. If the angle was too high it would fly over the target. If it angle was too low the spear would fall short.

3 Success! The gladiator hit the target and is ready to use a spear in combat.

CHAPTER FOUR

STAYING ALIVE IN THE ARENA

The main strategy for gladiators in the arena was simple: don't lose. For a gladiator, losing a fight usually meant losing his life. There were few rules in the arena. Tricky moves and blows from behind were not allowed. But otherwise gladiators had to be ready for anything.

Mock Battles

Gladiators didn't always fight one-on-one. Sometimes huge mock battles between gladiator "armies" filled the arena. During these battles, heavyweight gladiators often used a move called the "tortoise." They held up their shields to form a protective shell around them.

Gladiators didn't always fight other gladiators. Sometimes they fought wild and dangerous animals such as bulls, lions, or tigers to entertain the crowd.

Lightweight gladiators spaced themselves around the edges of the group. Some hurled spears called *hastas* into a battle from a distance. Others used their speed and mobility to strike quickly and then back off. A few lightweight gladiators, known as *essedari*, fought with heavy spears from fast-moving chariots. The chariots' speed allowed the spears to be thrown far and fast.

Fights between secutors and retiarii were very popular in ancient Rome. The two gladiator types had a perfect balance of speed and power against each other.

One-on-One Strategies

One of the most popular gladiator matchups was the retiarius vs. the secutor. The retiarius was popular because his weapons were so unusual. He could use his weighted net as a thrown weapon. But to be effective, he had to throw it at the correct **trajectory** to tangle up the secutor. He first swung it around to keep his enemy at a distance. He then tossed it at his enemy, hoping to tangle up his opponent's feet or weapons.

If the retiarius was successful with the net, he could then use his trident. The long weapon allowed him to attack from beyond the reach of the secutor's blade. He would use his speed to gain momentum and thrust the trident into his opponent's body.

The trident could also be used as a **projectile** weapon. But if the retiarius threw it, he would be without his main weapon. A skilled opponent could possibly kill him before he could pick the trident up again.

The secutor's main strategy was to stay behind his shield and wait for the retiarius to get close. One way a secutor could take out the enemy's trident was to deflect an attack with his shield. Then when the enemy was off balance, he could make a counter attack. The secutor didn't need much speed for his attack. His strength combined with his sharp gladius would be enough to strike a killing blow.

trajectory—the path of an object as it flies through the air

projectile—an object that is thrown or shot through the air

Sword Strategies

Most gladiators knew how to fight with a gladius. The warriors based their sword strategies on the opponents they faced and the weapons they used.

Thrusting

Thrusting attacks focused the force of the attack into the sword's sharp point. The warrior first crouched down to lower his center of gravity. He then created momentum and force by jumping up and forward. Thrusting attacks were best for piercing enemy armor and flesh.

Cutting and Slashing

The wide space in an arena provided a gladiator with plenty of room to swing his blade. This allowed him to put strength and speed into his attacks. Cutting and slashing attacks were best for fighting faster and lightly armored opponents.

Entertaining the Crowd

Gladiators might have been the rock stars of Rome, but they weren't soldiers. Their goal wasn't always to kill their enemies. Their job was to put on a good show for the crowd and the Emperor.

Running. Hitting. Cutting. Thrusting. Throwing. Gladiator fights were balanced with different science concepts to even the odds. One fighter was big and slow, but had heavy armor and weapons. Another had little protection, but was fast and could strike his enemy quickly. Whoever used science to his best advantage usually lived to fight another day.

agility (uh-JIL-uh-tee)—the ability to move in a quick and easy way

center of gravity (SEN-tur UHV GRAV-uh-tee)—the point at which a person or object can balance

deflect (di-FLEKT)—to cause something to go in a different direction

disperse (dis-PURS)—to spread out over a wide area

force (FORS)—energy or strength

kinetic energy (ki-NET-ik EN-ur-jee)—the energy of a moving object

mass (MASS)—the amount of material in an object

mobility (moh-BIL-uh-tee)—the ability to move quickly and easily

momentum (moh-MEN-tuhm)—the amount of force in a moving object determined by the object's mass and speed

physics (FIZ-iks)—science that studies matter, energy, force, and motion

potential energy (puh-TEN-shuhl EN-ur-jee)—energy stored in an object, waiting to be released

projectile (pruh-JEK-tuhl)—an object that is thrown or shot through the air

stamina (STAM-uh-nuh)—the energy and strength to keep doing something for a long time

trajectory (truh-JEK-tuh-ree)—the path of an object as it flies through the air

Critical Thinking Using the Common Core

1. Strength, force, movement, and speed were all part of a gladiator's life. How do you use these science ideas in your life every day? (Integration of Knowledge and Ideas)

2. Heavyweight and lightweight gladiators used different types of weapons, armor, and fighting styles. If you were a gladiator, which class would fit you best? What kinds of equipment would you have and how would you use it? (Key Ideas and Details)

Read More

Caper, William. *Gladiators: A Guide to the Deadly Warriors.* History's Greatest Warriors. North Mankato, Minn.: Capstone Press, 2012.

Dillard, Sheri. *Roman Gladiators.* Ancient Warriors. Mankato, Minn.: Child's World Publishing, 2015.

O'Brian, Pliny. *Gladiators: Battling in the Arena.* History's Greatest Warriors. New York: Cavendish Square Publishing, 2015.

Internet Sites

FactHound offers a safe, fun way to find Internet sites related to this book. All of the sites on FactHound have been researched by our staff.

Here's all you do:
Visit *www.facthound.com*
Type in this code: 9781491481295

 Check out projects, games and lots more at **www.capstonekids.com**